for men only

discussion guide

a companion to the bestseller about
the inner lives of women

shaunti and jeff feldhahn

with Brian Smith

MULTNOMAH
BOOKS

FOR MEN ONLY DISCUSSION GUIDE
PUBLISHED BY MULTNOMAH BOOKS
12265 Oracle Boulevard, Suite 200
Colorado Springs, Colorado 80921
A division of Random House Inc.

Scripture quotations are taken from the Holy Bible, New Living Translation, copyright © 1996. Used by permission of Tyndale House Publishers Inc., Wheaton, Illinois 60189. All rights reserved.

ISBN 978-1-59052-989-8

MULTNOMAH is a trademark of Multnomah Books and is registered in the U.S. Patent and Trademark Office. The colophon is a trademark of Multnomah Books.

Printed in the United States of America
2007—First Edition

10 9 8 7 6 5 4 3 2 1

Contents

1 Rethinking Random 1
    Why you need a new map of the female universe

2 The Deal Is Never Closed 8
    *Why her "I do" will always mean "Do you?"—and
    what to do about it*

3 Windows...Open! 18
    *What you should know about the fabulous female brain
    (a guide for lower life forms)*

4 Your Real Job Is Closer to Home 27
    *How your provider/protector instinct can leave
    her feeling more unsafe and less cared for*

5 Listening *Is* the Solution 37
    *Why her feeling about the problem is the problem,
    and how to fix your urge to fix*

6 With Sex, Her "No" Doesn't Mean You 47
    *How her desires are impacted by her unique wiring,
    and why your ego shouldn't be*

7 The Girl in the Mirror 57
    *What the little girl inside your woman is dying to hear
    from you—and how to guard your answer well*

8 The Man She Had Hoped to Marry 67
    What the woman who loves you most, most wants you to know

Appendix: The *For Men Only* Resolutions 73

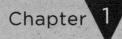

Chapter 1

RETHINKING
RANDOM

*Why you need a new map
of the female universe*

Greetings, my fellow semiconfused male. I imagine you've picked up this book in search of some help navigating the wild, seemingly unpredictable inner world of women. Or—let's be frank—because the woman in your life "strongly suggested" that you needed such help.

When it comes to relationship stuff, I've felt about as lost as a guy can get. Then my wife became a surprise best-selling author on relationships. Ironic, huh? Eventually I got enlisted to help research and explain these mysterious beings called women in a way that ordinary mortals like me could grasp. To my surprise, I discovered that women are a lot easier to understand than I thought, and I shared what I learned in the book *For Men Only: A Straightforward Guide to the Inner Lives of Women* coauthored with my wife, Shaunti.

The overwhelmingly positive responses from guys across the country confirmed my suspicions: despite all the jokes about "clueless" men, most of us genuinely want to be better husbands or boyfriends; we simply need a little help in figuring out how. And that's the basic idea behind this discussion guide: using the insights from *For Men Only* to identify simple changes that can make huge differences in our relationships.

Where Are We Headed?

The chart below outlines the six most important findings from the *For Men Only* research into how women are wired. The column on the left, "Our Surface Understanding," notes what we guys generally know or tend to assume about women. The column on the right, "What That Means in Practice," highlights an often surprising truth behind those assumptions—and how that truth plays out in everyday life. These are the key ideas we'll work through in the following chapters.

Our Surface Understanding	What That Means in Practice
Women need to feel loved.	Even if your relationship is great, your mate likely has a fundamental insecurity about your love—and when that insecurity is triggered, she may respond in ways that confuse or dismay you until she feels reassured.
Women are emotional.	Women deal with multiple thoughts and emotions from their past and present all the time, at the same time—and these can't be easily dismissed.
Women want security—in other words, financial security.	Your woman needs emotional security and closeness with you so much that she will endure financial insecurity to get it.

She doesn't want you to fix it; she just wants you to listen.	When she is sharing an emotional problem, her feelings and her desire to be heard are much more important than the problem itself.
She doesn't want much sex; she must not want me.	Physically, women tend to crave sex less often than men do—and it is usually not related to your desirability.
She wants to look attractive.	Inside your smart, secure wife lives a little girl who deeply needs to know that you find her beautiful—and that you only have eyes for her.

These findings, based on the results of a groundbreaking survey of women, provide us with a map of sorts. I used to think of women as a mapless swamp, but now I'm seeing that they're not nearly as foggy as I thought and that a few simple things can transform our relationships for the better and help us meet the deepest needs of the women in our lives.

I hope you'll find this guide helpful whether you're married, dating, or single. You'll notice pretty quickly that I use the words "woman," "wife," and "girlfriend" somewhat interchangeably (except when we talk about sex, because I agree with the Bible's plan for reserving sex for marriage). My main goal is to help you apply these ideas in your romantic relationship, but I think you'll find they will also help you relate better to other women in your life, like your daughter, as well as female relatives, fellow workers, and friends.

Personally, while I haven't mastered the ability to always apply what I've learned (actually, far from always), by putting these findings to work in my marriage I have experienced far greater peace in my relationship with Shaunti. So I'm pretty confident that with the woman you love, you can too.

How to Use This Guide

You'll be glad to know that we designed this as a guy-friendly resource that has been test-driven by real-world groups of men, that you can explore on your own or use as a helpful guide in a discussion group.

Each chapter corresponds to a chapter subject in the main book:

- Chapter 2: Reassurance
- Chapter 3: Emotions
- Chapter 4: Security
- Chapter 5: Listening
- Chapter 6: Sex (You can try bribing your leader to start with this chapter.)
- Chapter 7: Beauty
- Chapter 8: "You are my hero"

Each chapter has basically the same layout. Among other features you'll find...

- a Recap of the chapter
- a Key Questions section for discussion and/or personal reflection
- a Real World case study with follow-up questions to help you learn the skill of understanding what a woman is thinking
- A Woman's Perspective and A Man's Response—a comment that reflects a woman's thinking about the subject at hand, and a chance for you to respond (in the relative safety of your own home or surrounded by guys who understand)

- the Weekly Challenge—practical suggestions for how to actually *apply* what you're learning about the woman you love
- On the Home Front: Living It with Her—a standalone section that equips you to talk with your wife about what you're learning and seek her input (she's gonna *love* this—and I promise it won't be too painful for you)

Just to be clear: this guide is not like the instructions for installing a dishwasher. There're no step 1, step 2, and so on. You should mix and match the different elements, using those that best suit your needs or the format of your group. Your discussion will probably go deeper and be most effective if you don't try to accomplish everything in each chapter.

For example, in a small-group setting of, say, six to ten men, some guys might be intent on learning the skill of "reading her mind" and therefore want to work through the Real World case studies, while others may feel they'll get the most benefit from the Weekly Challenges. Or if your time is limited, your group might decide to cover only three Key Questions from each chapter. I'd encourage you to start with an Introductory Week and work out a plan that will sufficiently challenge each guy without intimidating those of us who don't usually talk about such things.

Even in a larger group you may not want to tackle all the elements unless you can devote more than one session to each subject. The activities and questions in this discussion guide might be simply starting points as you add creative elements of your own, such as movie clips or icebreaker activities. You can find more ideas for organizing various types of groups around this discussion guide at our website: www.formenonly book.com.

No matter how your group is organized, you'll want to keep one essential in mind: From the first meeting to the last, confidentiality must be carefully guarded. What's shared in the group stays in the group.

Yes, This Guide Is Biased

Sometimes, as you work and talk through the book and guide, you may feel that you're being treated unfairly. "It seems like all the responsibility is on me," I can hear you groan. "Where's equal time for her to learn about *my* needs?" Well, all that's covered in another book called *For Women Only* and its companion discussion guide.

I've purposefully kept this discussion guide focused on what *you* need to know in order to understand the inner workings of that enigma called "woman." It's not supposed to help you change her; rather, it is supposed to help you change and improve yourself. And just so you know, I've been pleasantly surprised—shocked, even—to find out just how simple most of this stuff is. It's not rocket science, and I've seen firsthand that applying these simple truths will result in incalculable benefits for *both* of you.

As you work through the book, the most powerful discoveries you're likely to make are that you're not alone in your struggles and that it's not only your wife who's "weird" in these ways. (Did I say "weird"? I meant "extraordinary.") Not only that, your relational challenges are normal. Really. And realizing that you're not alone is half the battle.

So let's remember we're all in this together as we accept our first Weekly Challenge:

<u>Weekly Challenge:</u> This week, identify which, if any, of the six revelations on the chart you're already responding to effectively. Which is the most likely to require changes in your life?

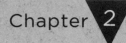

Chapter 2

THE DEAL IS NEVER CLOSED

Why her "I do" will always mean "Do you?"—and what to do about it

Weekly Challenge Report: Did all the revelations listed in the chart on pages 2–3 catch you off guard? If not, in which areas are you already doing pretty well at supporting the woman in your life? Which area needs the most work?

Recap

Even if your relationship is great, your mate likely has a fundamental insecurity about your love. Her feelings of insecurity are surprisingly frequent, intensely painful, and—to the male mind—paradoxically resistant to logic. When her insecurity is triggered by conflict between you, your silence, your absence, or stress in her life, she may respond in ways that confuse or dismay you. But when you're clued in, those puzzling behaviors serve as red warning lights, signaling you to respond to her need by verbally reassuring her of your love and by actively pursuing her to *show* that you value her.

"We're not talking here about what she knows logically, *but rather about the* feeling *that rises up when something has triggered it…. And it is this feeling that we need to take seriously."* —*Jeff, FMO, p. 29*

"You know that record that's always running in a guy's head about providing? Well, we have the same fundamental concern about our relationship all the time." —*quote from a woman, FMO, p. 31*

"A woman is likely to experience an undercurrent of emotional insecurity in her relationship even if you and I are totally innocent of intent, injury, or error…. But that doesn't mean we can't be part of the solution." —*Jeff, FMO, pp. 36–37*

Key Questions

Throughout this discussion guide, you'll find space to note your responses to questions, just in case you're a buttoned-down, fill-in-the-blanks kind of guy. But please consider that *optional*.

1. What idea in this chapter did you find most challenging and why?

2. Every woman is unique. What signals might your wife or girl-friend be sending that would indicate she's feeling insecure about your love? Playing detective, what words or body language do you think might communicate her need?

3. Describe an instance when your wife needed to be reassured of your love but you missed the opportunity. (This assumes you've picked up on those signals at least once.) Contrast the outcome of that scenario with a time you recognized her need and responded well.

4. What words or actions have worked best for you in reassuring and pursuing your wife or girlfriend? Now that the rest of us guys are completely in awe of you, what's something new you might try or, better yet, get one of the other guys in the group to try out first?

5. The apostle Paul advised married couples: "Each man must love his wife as he loves himself, and the wife must respect her husband" (Ephesians 5:33). If you actively look for ways to reassure and pursue the woman you love, in what ways might that affect her respect for you?

THE REAL WORLD

During their six years of marriage, Blake's love for Nicole had deepened with each day. He loved how she cared for their two energetic children and was proud that his income enabled her to stay home with them. However, over the past few months he'd noticed that Nicole seemed increasingly negative and critical, not just toward him but about everything in her world. If anything, he thought, she should find her circumstances *more* uplifting. Their second child had just graduated from diapers, and after years of investing long hours in his audio and video production business, their financial situation finally seemed relatively secure.

One evening he asked her to be sure to wash a particular shirt for a meeting two days away. Nicole blew up. "So I'm just your maid now, is that it?" Surprised and

angry, Blake initially felt like shutting down and not talking. He fought that urge, however, and determined to
find out what was wrong. But when he followed her
upstairs, she told him to go away and then closed the
door to the bedroom.

Case Study Questions

Note to participants: The main goal of the case studies is to help
you gain a critical skill that many of us lack, namely understanding what on earth a woman is thinking. That said, if you
find yourself completely flummoxed by the case study questions,
you can get the inside track on the woman's perspective from a
cheat sheet created by Shaunti that is available on our *For Men
Only* website: www.formenonlybook.com. Group leaders may
want to print out the cheat sheet to have on hand for the discussion, but you'll find that your skill in "reading her mind"
improves most if you wrestle with the questions *before* you resort
to the cheat sheet.

1. What might have been some of the reasons for Nicole's growing
   discouragement?

2. Put yourself in Nicole's shoes. (Not her favorite pumps though; they can really put a strain on a guy's lower back.) What might her overreaction to Blake's laundry request signal about her feelings toward (a) her daily responsibilities and (b) Blake?

3. Stay in Nicole's shoes. (They accent that cute little handbag.) What do you think she wanted from Blake in the midst of this conflict? What might have been her subconscious motive—the "payoff" she hoped to receive—for pushing him away?

4. What would be the best thing that Blake could say or do that evening and over the next few days to improve his relationship with Nicole? The worst?

A Woman's Perspective: "It was when a male co-worker told me he was attracted to me, because I was so funny and fun to be around, that I pinpointed what I've been so hungry for from my husband. I have no interest in this other guy. But even so, his words of affirmation felt like a shower in the desert. Ever since then, I go to bed almost every night deeply disappointed that my husband won't simply tell me he loves me… without my begging him to."

A Man's Response: Does it seem unfair or illogical that this woman won't just come right out and tell her husband what she needs from him? Why do you suppose it's so important to her that he think of it himself? How do you see this perspective mirrored in your own relationship?

> <u>Weekly Challenge:</u> (1) Put up your relationship antennas for the next few days. (Trust me, these are standard issue for all guys, though most of us think that ours got left off at the factory.) Watch for possible signs that your wife or girlfriend may be having an episode of feeling uncertain of your love for her. (2) Even if you don't pick up any signals of insecurity, think of two specific ways to reassure her of your love—one through words and one through actions. (3) Try them and notice what happens.

Someone Once Said...

"Sometimes something worth doing is worth overdoing."
—David Letterman

The BIG Idea

One main idea I'm taking away from this week's discussion is...

One way I plan to apply this insight to my relationship is...

ON THE HOME FRONT:
LIVING IT WITH HER

Note: This section will help you talk with your wife or girlfriend about the insights you're gaining when it comes to her needs and concerns, and can be used as a standalone tool even if you are not going through the other sections with a group.

Now that you realize how likely it is that the woman in your life has an underlying concern about losing your love—and that you can prevent some of that insecurity by reassuring her consistently and regularly—the trick is to figure out how to give that reassurance in a way that speaks to her heart. The quickest way—though for us guys, perhaps not the most painless—is to come right out and ask.

Wake Up Your Inner Hero

If you're feeling a bit hesitant about this whole talking thing, that just shows your testosterone is at a healthy level. Who wants to open himself up for potential criticism? But even if she's shut you out in the past, the fact that you're man enough to risk this conversation should serve as evidence of your love and earn you some brownie points. Remember that if she pushes you away, she's really hoping you'll follow.

Take the Plunge

Here are a few suggestions to get the conversation started. Chances are, all you'll need to do is ask a question or two and she'll gladly take it from there.

- Since I honestly never question whether you love me, I didn't realize that you might sometimes wonder whether I really love you. Just for the record, I do! Since examples will help me understand how you may feel here, what are some things I might say or do that make you worried about us, or about whether I truly love you? For example, what does it feel like for you when we have a conflict and I shut down?

- What are a few of the things that I say and do that most make you feel reassured that I *do* love you and will always be here for you?

- I think that when you say or do this, _____, that's a signal that you could use some reassurance of my love for you; am I right? What other clues am I missing?

- When we're arguing or frustrated with each other, how can I reassure you of my love while still giving myself time to process what's happening?

- When you are upset and withdraw from me, do you ever hope that I'll come after you?

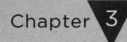

Chapter 3

WINDOWS...
OPEN!

What you should know about the fabulous female brain (a guide for lower life forms)

<u>Weekly Challenge Report:</u> What signs did you detect that your wife or girlfriend needed reassurance of your love...or was the microwave interfering with your relational antennas? Did you try new (or old) ways to reassure her? How'd it go?

Recap

Men generally focus on one thing at a time, compartmentalizing other thoughts and feelings for later consideration. But most women experience multiple thoughts and emotions at the same time that can't easily be dismissed. Many women are blindsided regularly by negative, unresolved thoughts and feelings from the recent or far past. Sudden shifts in topic, introduction of "ancient history," or flashes of emotion often signal a past or current concern that keeps invading a woman's awareness even if she doesn't want it there. You can help "close those windows" by nondefensively allowing her to talk out and/or resolve whatever concern is popping up—or even by taking some action to resolve it for her.

"If all men are truly visual and can't help it, then I think they should please understand that women are truly verbal and can't help it. For example, the things men say to us are in mental tape archives and are as real today as they were the moment they were spoken." —quote from a woman, FMO, p. 60

"Maybe she's not trying to hassle you by wanting to talk about fourteen things as soon as you come through the door after work. She really does have fourteen files open and running." —Jeff, FMO, p. 69

"If she brings up old wounds, she may not be holding on to a grudge, but actually trying to process through it so she can resolve it, close the window, and let it go." —Jeff, FMO, p. 69

Key Questions

Remember, written responses to questions are *optional.* Respond in a way that best helps you absorb new insights. Yes, chainsaw-carving and hedge-trimming provide great opportunities to think things through, but please hold off until after the group discussion.

1. If another guy asked you for advice about the working of the female mind, how would you summarize the idea you found most compelling in this chapter?

2. Think of something your wife or girlfriend has said or done in the past few weeks that sent you spinning at the time but that now makes more sense in light of this chapter. How did you respond then? If you were given a do-over (don't you wish!), what would you do differently in light of your new-found understanding?

3. In your own experience, what other evidence have you seen that women are constantly juggling multiple thoughts and feel-ings and can't always close those that are bothering them?

4. Describe a typical situation in which the woman you love might have trouble closing a particular mental window. The next time this occurs, how could you step up to help her resolve her concerns and close the window? (Hint: "Rebooting her" is not a valid answer.)

THE REAL WORLD

The evening after the infamous Laundry Incident (see chapter 2, "The Real World"), Blake found Nicole in a calmer mood. She listened as he expressed how grateful he always was for her work around the house, especially the laundry. He gave her a hug as he said, "I'm so amazed at how you keep up with everything."

They sat on the couch, and Nicole leaned against him. "I guess I need to hear that kind of thing a lot more often," she told him. "It's a pleasant relief from the criticism I keep getting from your mother."

Surprised, Blake fell quiet. *Where's this coming from?* he wondered. He knew his mom had made some comment months ago to Nicole about her responsibility to create a peaceful haven in their home. But his mom

lived across the country and had no way of knowing
how Nicole was handling the household day to day.

Blake had no idea what to say next. He'd thought he
was paying his wife a compliment. How in the world did
he step into this mess?

Case Study Questions

1. If Blake understood how the typical woman's mind works,
   what might Nicole's excavation of such "old news" suggest
   to him?

2. Imagine you're Nicole for a moment. What might be your
   motive—conscious or subconscious—for bringing up his
   mother's past comments?

3. You're still Nicole. Suppose Blake's next words are, "I don't
   understand why something Mom said so long ago is still bothering you. Can't you just let it go?" (If you find yourself winc-

ing, your relationship antennas are working great.) Why might those words send this conversation in a dangerous direction?

4. How would you advise Blake to respond to Nicole's expression of past and present pain to help her close this window?

5. Even better, what *action* might Blake take to close the window for her?

A Woman's Perspective: "I wish that I had the ability to share with my husband all the thoughts that are constantly running through my head that I need to talk out—and that he had the capacity to listen without his head exploding."

A Man's Response: How might an understanding husband express his empathy if his wife spoke these words? Given his limited capacity to endure—excuse me, I mean *absorb*—multiple conversations, how could he still help her process and resolve her concerns?

Weekly Challenge: (1) This week, take note of the variety of activities and concerns your wife or girlfriend feels responsible for. Picture how her related thoughts and feelings must pile up inside, and consider how your affirmation might help prevent your being buried by her occasional verbal avalanches. (2) Look for an open window that might be bothering her, and see if you can find a way to help her resolve it.

Someone Once Said...

"Women always worry about the things that men forget; men always worry about the things women remember." —author unknown

The BIG Idea

One main idea I'm taking away from this week's discussion is...

One way I plan to apply this insight to my relationship is...

ON THE HOME FRONT: LIVING IT WITH HER

The fact that a woman's brain is wired for multitasking, endures pop-up feelings from the past, and can't be easily shut off explains why we sometimes find it so hard to keep up with a rapid-fire conversation or feel ambushed by her "unwillingness" to set aside a concern. But how can we put this new understanding to practical use?

Wake Up Your Inner Hero

Rather than surrendering to your fight-or-flight instinct when your wife or girlfriend brings up an issue from the past, you might consider whether she, too, has been ambushed by its sudden appearance. Perhaps the problem is stalking her, not you, and she needs your help to get rid of it once and for all.

As you lead the charge to hunt down and kill—uh, I mean, resolve—the problem, don't be surprised if she suddenly shifts into talking about something completely different. At that point, you have two choices. You can try to shift topics with her—tricky for many guys—hoping that perhaps this new trail leads to the heart of the problem. Or you can gently remind her that you're working with a one-thing-at-a-time brain and suggest dealing with the original issue before moving on to the next.

Take the Plunge

The woman in your life will be thrilled—and possibly amused—to know that you're interested in how and what she thinks. Why not try out one or two of the following conversation starters to gain even more insight about how her mind works?

- Is it true that women tend to have many things running through their minds all at the same time? What's in *your* brain right now?

- When you mention a concern to me and I respond with, "Just don't worry about it," what usually happens in your mind? Are you able to push that concern aside? How would you prefer I respond in that situation?

- Can you give me an example of a time when you had an open window that I *didn't* help you close? of a time when I did?

- What top concern keeps popping back into your thoughts these days, and how can I help you resolve it?

- Do you have any suggestions for how we could find a way to help you regularly download by telling me what's weighing on your mind without blowing my mental circuits? (This question may help cut down on those exhausting, after-the-lights-go-out conversations where you get in trouble for snoring in the middle of her heartfelt revelations.)

Chapter 4

YOUR REAL JOB IS CLOSER TO HOME

How your provider/protector instinct can leave her feeling more unsafe and less cared for

<u>Weekly Challenge Report:</u> What did you observe this week about your wife's or girlfriend's internal multitasking abilities? (And you thought making a sandwich while watching a football game was an accomplishment.) What insights did this give you regarding her sometimes chaotic inner life and what she might need from you? Were you able to help her close the window on any unresolved issues? How?

Recap

While most men think that a woman wants financial security, what she wants even more is emotional security. That is, she wants to feel close to you, to know that she's your non-work-time priority, to know you're committed to her, and to have you involved at home. And although she does want financial security, wants you to be fulfilled in your work, and appreciates your efforts to provide, she'd willingly endure financial struggles if that's what it took to have more of you (such as if you wanted a lower-paying, more family-friendly job). Fortunately, building emotional security and closeness is easier than you might think. Making small gestures of love and spending discretionary hours with her and at home instead of working overtime will go a long way.

"How could any man ever think we'd choose money over him?"
—quote from a woman, FMO, p. 78

"Your wife wants to be your love and *your best friend.... Living in the same house and even having sex doesn't necessarily mean that she feels close to you." —Jeff, FMO, p. 81*

"A wife does not *expect her husband to spend every off-the-job hour with her. But to feel emotionally secure, she can't feel that he's consistently choosing other time priorities over her." —Jeff, FMO, p. 85*

Key Questions

1. What insight served as your biggest *Aha!* from this chapter?

2. Describe a situation in which your wife or girlfriend is most likely to complain that she doesn't get enough of you. What underlying issue or circumstance seems to provoke this comment most often?

3. If she were able to converse in Man-Talk (Manglish? Mannese? Mandarin?), how might she express her desire in a way that made sense to you?

4. What actions or words on your part seem to satisfy her need for connection? How can you tell those efforts are successful? Do they have to be exhausting and difficult to do in order to be effective?

THE REAL WORLD

Back in the early days when Blake was building his business, Nicole told him that the hardest thing about it was not having him around because of the long hours he had to put in. She regularly said she missed their time together but wanted him to achieve his dream. Thankful for her patience and understanding, Blake assured her things would change once the business was established and he could hire some help.

Over the past few years clients had flocked to his door, and he had gradually acquired a small support staff. But as his client base grew and the projects became more complex and challenging, Blake felt a need to continue working just as hard.

Shortly before their first child was born, the couple had felt confident enough in their cash flow from the business to move out of their apartment and purchase their first house. More recently, after baby number two arrived, Blake was delighted to buy a brand-new minivan in the make Nicole wanted. So he didn't understand why she seemed increasingly dissatisfied with the hours he was still keeping and kept bugging him about spending more time at home with her and the kids. Frustrated, he wondered why Nicole didn't seem to recognize that the money for mortgage and car payments didn't grow on trees.

Case Study Questions

1. What is Blake's greatest concern? In particular, what does he think Nicole expects of him?

2. Now put yourself in Nicole's shoes. What was her highest priority (the thing she wanted the most) when she and Blake had very little money and lived in an apartment? What sacrifice did she make during those early years? How long did she expect that situation to last?

3. Stay in Nicole's shoes. What is her highest priority now that Blake's business is established? Has it changed in any way?

4. As Nicole looks at Blake's working so hard and being away from the family, what might *she* be thinking about what *he's* thinking? Remember, you're still looking at the world from *her* perspective. What signal might his long hours away be sending to her?

5. Beyond her highest priority, what might her main concern for him be?

6. What steps could they take to address the concerns of each person without either having to sacrifice what's important to each of them?

A Woman's Perspective: "My husband's layoff was the best thing that ever happened to us. Before, I got 'quality time' with him about twice a year on lavish weekend getaways. He was depressed at first. Now he makes half as much and things have been tight, but he enjoys his work. And he's always home by six and has weekends off. He now sees how good this low-stress lifestyle is for him. It's *really* good for me, too. I never knew that he felt I needed material things more than his happiness in his job or our time together."

A Man's Response: Do you have trouble believing that a woman might actually *mean* what this woman says? Why? What evidence have you seen that confirms or contradicts her comments? Since we as men are wired to provide, might we sometimes give more notice to their comments about financial desires than their comments about wanting us around? Do you think your wife or girlfriend might share this woman's perspective? What signals have you seen that she might be willing to trade some current or future comfort for more time and enjoyment together now?

Weekly Challenge: (1) Think of two new ideas [or old ideas you haven't used for a while—like, since you were dating] for simple ways to draw closer to the woman in your life. To be valid, they have to be the sort of thing you could see yourself doing consistently without becoming exhausted, but also be something more personal than sorting your open-end wrenches together. (2) Choose one of these ideas to try out this week and notice how she responds. (3) Optional: Not everyone needs to make a radical change—like moving to a smaller house or changing to a less-demanding

job—in order to bring life back into balance,
but you may want to talk with your wife about
whether such measures should be considered
for the health of your marriage and family.

Someone Once Said...

"If women didn't exist, all the money in the world would have no
meaning." —Aristotle Onassis

The BIG Idea

One main idea I'm taking away from this week's discussion is…

One way I plan to apply this idea in my relationship is…

ON THE HOME FRONT: LIVING IT WITH HER

So how can we fulfill our manly need to work and provide financially for our loved ones while still meeting our woman's need for our time and attention? More to the point, will the woman in your life be satisfied with simple expressions of affection and intimacy, or is her craving for emotional security a bottomless pit you can never hope to fill?

Wake Up Your Inner Hero

When a woman experiences a season of insecurity about her man's commitment, she often becomes clingy and possessive. Under her smothering attentions, your masculine brain may shift into panic mode and urge you to "Run, Forrest, run!"

If you can summon the courage not only to resist that urge but also to draw closer, you may be surprised at how little it takes to meet her need for emotional security. She'll likely respond with warmth and affirmation that seem out of proportion to the small gestures you've made. And when you regularly take a bit of initiative to build that sense of closeness, you'll almost certainly find that you both have a greater sense of freedom and satisfaction in your relationship.

Take the Plunge

The key to achieving this balance is identifying how the woman in your life defines security. By posing one or two of the following questions to her, I think you'll quickly learn whether your ideas are on the right track.

- Do you ever wonder if my work is more important to me than you are?
- What are some things I already do that let you know you're a priority in my life? What other little things could I do to help you feel loved and secure?

Additional questions, only for those who are married:

- What are your nonnegotiables when it comes to our financial or material needs? What are your nonnegotiables in our relationship?
- Do you think we need to make any changes in our family priorities—and resulting changes in our lifestyle—to help strengthen our relationship and our family? How can we make that happen?

Chapter 5

LISTENING *IS* THE SOLUTION

Why her feeling about the problem is the problem, and how to fix your urge to fix

Weekly Challenge Report: Describe the ideas you came up with to draw closer to your wife or girlfriend. Which one did you take for a test drive, and how successful was it? (We know something worked; you didn't get all the lipstick off.) What simple tips would you suggest to other guys who are struggling in this area? If you and your wife discussed the work hours versus lifestyle conundrum, what did you learn about her perspective?

Recap

When a woman voices an emotional concern, a man's first instinct is to set aside her emotions, identify the technical problem, and fix it. But what she needs first is for us to give her our full attention, set aside the technical problem, and instead listen to and validate what she's feeling about it…as odd as that feels to us. By restating her concern and telling her it's okay to feel that way, you will actually fix a problem for her—the emotional one that needs to be addressed before she will be interested in actually tackling the technical one. As you learn to listen in the way she needs, you may sometimes feel that she's blaming you, when in fact she probably appreci-ates you more than you realize.

"Listening…is an active practice of identifying her feelings, considering what she's really saying, and listening for the story behind the story."
—Jeff, FMO, p. 110

"Instead of filtering out her feelings to concentrate on the problem, we need to practice filtering out the problem so we can concentrate on her feelings about it." —Jeff, FMO, p. 112

"Men don't realize the value of affirming our feelings when they seem irrational or out of proportion to them. If a man could just grasp the value of that, he could cut arguments or long discussion times in half."
—quote from a woman, FMO, p. 114

Key Questions

1. As you make your way around the listening diamond (described on page 107 of FMO) toward home plate, where do you most often run into trouble and why? (And did you

have as much trouble as I did adapting to this definition of "home run"?)

2. Are you often surprised by negative responses when you offer solutions to your wife's or girlfriend's concerns without first acknowledging her feelings? Describe a time when you thought you were being helpful but your wife or girlfriend accused you of not listening or caring. What response do you think she was looking for?

3. You'll score ten bonus points if you can describe a similar occasion when she thanked you for listening well. What specifically did you do right in that instance?

4. What distractions most often compete for your attention when your wife or girlfriend wants to talk? What's your new strategy for giving her your full attention?

5. Those four little words—"We need to talk"—can instantly drain our energy, even before the conversation begins. What approach would work best in your relationship for giving your wife or girlfriend the verbal processing time she needs without overloading your own circuits? How could you let her know about your listening limitations and how working within those constraints might help your relationship?

THE REAL WORLD

One Sunday afternoon after settling the kids in their rooms for some quiet time, Blake turned on the TV to watch his team in the playoffs. A few minutes later Nicole plopped down beside him on the sofa and started talking about their toddler. "I just don't know what to do about Ethan. Every time I drop him off at

Sunday school, he cries and begs me not to leave. By the time I finally pry him loose and slip out the door, he's in hysterics. The teacher says he calms down within less than a minute...but should I be leaving him there at all? I wonder if I've done something that's making him feel insecure..."

Blake heard the smothered emotion in Nicole's voice and knew he needed to address something that was clearly troubling his wife.

He glanced sideways. "Should I try taking him to class instead?"

"Oh, just forget it," Nicole declared. "I'm sorry I even brought it up."

Case Study Questions

1. Being the sensitive and insightful guy you are, what mistakes do you think Blake might have made in this scenario? If he were familiar with the four listening bases identified on page 107 of FMO, what might have been his response when Nicole first started talking?

2. Put yourself in Nicole's place. What was the deeper issue underneath the concern she described? What is troubling her more than Ethan's actual behavior?

3. Stay in Nicole's place. (I'll let you get back to watching the game with Blake in a minute.) Can that troubled feeling be solved by good advice? What might alleviate her burden of concern?

4. Consider her last comment; does she really want Blake to drop the subject? If not, what is she hoping his next move will be?

5. If he does take the excuse to drop the subject (figuring he can get back to it after the game), what will Nicole assume about

his concern for her feelings? Is there any way Nicole can be reassured that he cares about her feelings and still understand that he can't quite concentrate on them until after the game?

A Woman's Perspective: "I would have been insulted if he had told me to just forgive my sister and let it go; that I can do by myself. What I couldn't do by myself was process my disappointment and feel okay about myself. Somehow he figured out how to walk through that with me. I was stunned. And delighted."

A Man's Response: When your wife or girlfriend tells you about a relationship conflict, what's usually your first impulse? How do you feel about the suggestion that you affirm her feelings even if you disagree with her assessment of the situation or believe she's overreacting? If this doesn't come naturally, what might help you figure out how to walk through the feelings with her?

Weekly Challenge: (1) This week, when the woman in your life voices an emotion-laden concern, take notice of your inner thoughts and feelings. How does your instinctive response line up with her needs, according to what you've learned in this chapter? If you find yourself feeling defensive, listen to hear whether you're really under attack or whether she's just processing aloud. (2) Watch for an opportunity to round the listening bases and head for home plate. How does she respond to your careful listening and affirming words?

Someone Once Said...

"Men and women belong to different species, and communications between them is a science still in its infancy." —Bill Cosby

The BIG Idea

One main idea I'm taking away from this week's discussion is...

One way I plan to apply this insight to my relationship is...

ON THE HOME FRONT: LIVING IT WITH HER

They say the way to a man's heart is through his stomach, but apparently the way to a woman's heart leads through the man's ears. Weird, huh? But to the woman in your life, listening equals love. Unfortunately, active listening is an energy-draining activity for most of us. So what's a guy to do?

Wake Up Your Inner Hero

The only way to build up our confidence that we can do this well is to practice our listening skills on a regular basis. The good news—or bad, depending on your perspective—is that on any given day our wives will give us multiple opportunities to do so. Each time we put down our fix-the-problem tools and reach into our focus-on-her-feelings kit, we'll find it easier to break free of those old habits that left us both so frustrated.

The first few times you work at real listening, she may not respond with instant appreciation. Perhaps she needs time to realize you're not going to get defensive or fall into the same old fix-the-issue pattern. The key is to remember that you're already her hero; she's coming to you for help because she values and needs your support.

Take the Plunge

You'll probably have many occasions this week to give your listening skills a workout, but engaging her in conversation on one or more of the following points will give you additional opportunities to put your new insights into practice.

- I'm trying to learn how to listen in the way you need me to. Can you give me an example of a time you shared something with me and felt I was more focused on fixing than on listening?

- What do you need to hear from me to know that I'm listening in a way that makes you feel cared for? (If what you hear involves listening to and acknowledging her feelings first, feel free to explain that that seems like a wimpy response to a lot of guys, as if you're not doing enough.)

- When you want to talk about issues in our relationship, I realize that sometimes I get kind of defensive, feeling like I'm always the one at fault. Am I jumping to conclusions, or is this really how you feel?

- What kind of signals should I watch for to know when you want me to help solve a problem versus when you just need me to hear you out?

Chapter 6

WITH SEX, HER "NO" DOESN'T MEAN YOU

How her desires are impacted by her unique wiring, and why your ego shouldn't be

Weekly Challenge Report: As you observed your own feelings about your wife's or girlfriend's concerns, were you able to set aside any initial defensiveness on your part? If so, what did you then learn about her true motivation? What feelings did you uncover as you listened for and acknowledged them, and how did she respond as you did so?

Recap

Most women tend to crave sex less often than men do, and it's usually *not* because the woman doesn't desire her husband. A woman's sexual wiring is distinctly different from a man's, including a different hormone mix, a more emotional (instead of visual) orientation, and a physical and mental need for anticipation time. Often she's as frustrated as you are by the sexual differences between you and would change those factors if she could. The good news is, just a few simple changes can propel you toward the kind of sexual relationship *both* of you want. These include building the day-to-day closeness she needs *outside* the bedroom, flirting with her (again, *outside* the bedroom) so she knows she's attractive and desirable and you'd choose her all over again, and letting her know what's on your menu for the evening well before you step *into* the bedroom.

"Most women do care about what their man wants. And they do care about sex. And they do want great sexual relationships with their husband." —Jeff, FMO, p. 122

"For guys, it seems, sex provides relief or escape from exhaustion. For women, we have to pull ourselves out of exhaustion in order to want to have sex." —quote from a woman, FMO, p. 129

"Where you might greatly desire her even though she was rude to you this morning, how you treated her this morning really matters.... For her, those two things—what's in her heart about you and how she can respond sexually—meld into one." —Jeff, FMO, p. 135

Key Questions

1. What's the most helpful insight you gained from this chapter about the physical aspects of a woman's sexual wiring? What about the emotional aspects?

2. Talking about sex can be one of the most difficult and embarrassing things for some guys. So I'll try to start out general. If you're willing to answer, feel free to elaborate as little or as much as you want. Which of the following best describes your sex life?

   a. I'm not married.
   b. What sex life?
   c. We have a few problems, but who doesn't?
   d. Uh…love it, but would love a little *more* of it.
   e. Generally, I'm pretty happy with life, if you know what I mean.

3. On a typical day, how would you describe your wife's attitude toward sex? How does this compare with her attitude once you're engaged in the act? What do you think explains this?

4. Think about one time when you knew your wife was really into it. You felt that she found you deeply desirable and expressed it through sex. What, if anything, did you say or do that helped lead to this outcome? What other circumstances might have contributed to her increased interest?

The Real World

All week, Blake had knocked off work early so he could work on the house with Nicole. First they painted his home office, and then they tackled the laborious job of papering the dining room. Blake didn't particularly care for the rose-flecked wallpaper, but he knew Nicole loved it. On Saturday, he bought a cheap origami kit he saw in a card-shop window and used it to make a paper box with a paper flower inside. He wrote "You're my perfect rose" on the flower petals. He called their baby-sitter from work on Monday to make arrangements for the following night.

Tuesday at lunchtime, he sent Nicole an e-mail: "Hey, hon, don't worry about dinner tonight. I've got a surprise for you. If you like it...maybe you can surprise me!" He left work at 4:30 and took the kids to the sitter's house, smiling mysteriously when Nicole asked what was going on. On the way back home, he picked up an order of Nicole's favorite Chinese food. During their refreshingly peaceful dinner, Blake gave her the origami box and flower. He didn't even get to open his fortune cookie before she dragged him to the couch and overpowered him.

Case Study Questions

Leader: At this point, allow a moment for group members to emerge out of their dazed silence. It will wear off after a minute or so.

1. Our man Blake is finally learning to think like a woman—and what a payoff! Why don't you try your hand at this rewarding skill by putting yourself in Nicole's place and making a list of each right thing our hero said and did, starting with the first sentence of the story. On your list, include (a) what did each action say to Nicole? and (b) how did it make her feel? Noticing a pattern?

2. Continue looking at this from Nicole's perspective. You see him take time off from work to spend time on something important to the family. Are you thinking about sex? Okay, now you're painting the home office with your husband and wallpapering the dining room. Are you thinking about sex? Now, on Tuesday imagine that Blake *doesn't send that e-mail* and still surprises you with the baby-sitter and the Chinese food and the origami rose. Are you thinking about sex? Remember, you're Nicole now, not Blake. *Without that e-mail, how might the evening have ended?*

3. Stay in Nicole's perspective if you possibly can. What happens in her thoughts and emotions once she gets that e-mail? (Does she start thinking about—and anticipating—something that wasn't on her mind before?) What difference do those new thoughts and feelings make to how she perceives Blake's thoughtfulness, right from the start of the evening?

4. In that vein, what are some reasons the e-mail didn't backfire and lead to the "you only think about one thing" accusation? What does that tell you about the context that most women need to be willing to be turned on?

A Woman's Perspective: "I love my husband all the time. And I love sex some of the time—that is, I love it once we get going. I wish he would make use of that all-the-time love we have to help me get to the some-of-the-time more often."

A Man's Response: What's your reaction to the idea that your wife needs warning or help to get interested in sex? Can you identify why you feel that way? What's the source of the expectation that "sex should be spontaneous"?

<u>Weekly Challenge:</u>

For married men: Look back at "A Guide for Ordinary Husbands" on pages 138–47 of FMO. Choose one of the eight pointers to focus on starting this week, recognizing it may take longer than one week to see results. How will you put it into practice, specifically? (That's a joke, fellas. We really don't want that much detail.)

For single and married men: This week, observe the messages the media and entertainment industry send about women's readiness for and interest in sex. Consider how those messages might impact your own expectations.

Someone Once Said...

"Women need a reason to have sex. Men just need a place."
—Billy Crystal

The BIG Idea

One main idea I'm taking away from this week's discussion is...

One way I plan to apply this insight to my relationship is...

ON THE HOME FRONT: LIVING IT WITH HER

Unfortunately, knowing the reasons your wife may have less interest in sex than you do—it's about her wiring, not your desirability—doesn't necessarily make them easier to take. Your sexual success with your wife is closely linked to your sense of self-esteem—and those needs don't just go away no matter how understanding you'd like to be. That's why those outside-the-bedroom efforts are more than worth the investment.

Wake Up Your Inner Hero

If you've been paying attention—and I know you have!—this chapter has probably already given you some ideas for how to get her warmed up to the idea of improving your sex life. But the memory of all those "Not tonight" responses may leave you feeling hesitant to talk openly with her about your needs. Who needs more rejection, right?

Believe it or not, it's very likely that she doesn't realize how her unresponsiveness affects you emotionally or how vulnerable you feel when you approach her for intimacy. Once she realizes that her "no" makes you feel undesirable and affects your confidence in other areas of your life, she may be much more willing to talk about how to address this emotional need in a way that works for *both* of you.

Take the Plunge

The best time to talk about your sex life is when (1) sex is not imminent and (2) you're both in a calm, receptive mood. Even then, don't be surprised if she makes a crack about your one-track mind. Once she hears that you truly care about meeting her emotional/sexual needs, not just your own needs, you'll both be on your way to more and better. Here are a few suggestions for learning how to better meet her needs so she can help with yours:

- If I don't bring it up, do you think about sex during the day? How often do you think about wanting sex if I haven't put the thought in your head or if it's not our usual time (Fair warning: the *typical* answer may be hard to hear, like, "Uh, never.")

- Can I tell you what sex means to me and how it makes me feel about myself *outside* the bedroom? (For a female-oriented summary, you can show her the sex chapter of *For Women Only*.)

- Does it make a difference in your emotional or physical interest level if you have some time to anticipate and start thinking about our being intimate? What suggestions do you have for how I could give you advance notice of how I'd love the evening to end—without making you feel like I was demanding something?

- When you say, "Not tonight," what's typically your reason? What can I do to help resolve that reason, and get us to "all systems go" more often?

- Most of us guys want to be intimate with our wives in order to feel closer, but I understand that most women want and need to feel close before they will be interested in sex. Do *you* feel that we need to build more closeness outside the bedroom? Can you give me some examples of what I do during the day that helps lay that foundation of feeling close? What else can I do to help us build that closeness?

Chapter 7

THE GIRL IN THE MIRROR

*What the little girl inside your woman
is dying to hear from you—and how
to guard your answer well*

Weekly Challenge Report:

For married men: What outcome have you seen
so far from putting last week's ideas into practice? Have you come to view your sexual relationship with your wife—and how she is wired—any
differently? How?

For single and married men: What messages
did you observe in the media about women and
sex? Which ideas seem to be grounded in reality
and which do not—and how will this affect your
future expectations?

Recap

A woman is unlikely to outgrow the little-girl need to hear that you—the man in her life—find her beautiful. She's bombarded daily with demeaning images and messages, and she has a deeply rooted need to be assured of your passionate attraction for her. You can counteract negative internal dialogue and external pressure by frequently, sincerely telling her she's beautiful to you, budgeting generously for her beautifying efforts, and deliberately avoiding the impulse to let your eyes or thoughts dwell on other women.

"Guys, we are divinely positioned to encourage and build up the woman we love; we can't be nodding off in the living room chair while the little girl twirls." —Jeff, FMO, p. 158

"A lot of women are so desperate for specific, honest compliments. We're dying of thirst for them…. One compliment can carry me for a long way." —quote from a woman, FMO, p. 159

"If a woman sees her husband's eyes also *affirming the beauty of other women, she ceases to feel special." —Jeff, FMO, pp. 166–67*

Key Questions

1. What insight in this chapter did you find most challenging? most helpful?

2. What's a typical way your wife or girlfriend might fish for your affirmation of her beauty? (If your answer is, "I have no idea what you're talking about," please stop and ask the group for immediate prayer.) What kind of responses have you given that seem to meet her hunger for affirmation? What kind of responses have backfired? What do you think makes the difference?

3. How about some advance planning? One of these days she's sure to ask your opinion about her appearance, and it's going to be one of the *scary* questions about some aspect you don't find quite so beautiful. How might you both affirm her and support her efforts at improvement—without digging yourself into a hole?

4. You know how much it would hurt your wife or girlfriend if you cheated on her sexually. Now consider Jesus's teaching: "Anyone who even looks at a woman with lust has already committed adultery with her in his heart" (Matthew 5:28). What steps can you take to guard against lustful eyes or thoughts (or to win the battle, if that's an issue you're

fighting already) and to protect that little girl inside the woman you love?

THE REAL WORLD

More than two years after the birth of their second child, Nicole still hadn't lost all her pregnancy weight. Blake noticed that she tended to dress quickly when he was present and seemed embarrassed about her body. She occasionally muttered comments about gravity taking a toll or about pregnancy having left its mark. When she said things like, "Now you're married to a fat old lady," or, "I wish I could be beautiful for you again," he cringed and protested stumblingly. In truth, he did wish she'd lose the excess weight, but he didn't know how to encourage her without causing further pain. Yet nothing could change the fact that he still became excited by her body, got lost in her deep brown eyes (especially when she smiled *that* smile), and constantly thought about making love with her—even if it was hard to find the time these days.

Case Study Questions

1. For a moment, put yourself in Nicole's place—not the grown-up Nicole, but the little girl twirling inside. First, feel her desperate internal need to be told she's pretty and affirmed for who she is—especially to hear it from the most important man in her life. Now look at the world through Nicole's eyes…at the countless media images of how women "should" look. How does Nicole now feel about *herself*? And what does she need even more from the most important man in her life?

2. Keeping in mind this need, if Nicole goes for a long time without hearing that her man finds her beautiful, what might she do to protect the hungry little girl inside? Have you seen your wife or girlfriend doing anything like this?

3. What would it feel like to Nicole if she noticed Blake's eyes lingering on another woman's figure? What message would play in her head? Alternatively, what if Blake turned away from other attractive women, communicating verbally or

through his actions that "I only have eyes for you"? How would this make her feel?

4. What do you think Nicole is longing to hear when she makes a disparaging comment about herself? Is there any downside to Blake's saying just that? Why or why not?

5. Imagine that you're Nicole's best female friend and that you've become aware of Blake's confusion about how he can encourage Nicole. What advice would you give Blake (be kind, now) that would help him resolve his conundrum?

A Woman's Perspective: "Maybe guys will understand car talk. It's like my ego—my spirit—is a Ferrari, and there's only one station in the world where it can get the fuel it needs. My husband is the station attendant there, and the highest octane fuel he could give me would be something like, 'You're amazing. I love looking at you and being with you.' Then there are the lower grades, such as, 'I like your hair that way,' or,

'That dress looks nice on you.' Those are helpful. But if he says nothing or says, 'You look fine,' it's as if I drove up with my gas gauge on empty, but the attendant came out, kicked the tires, said, 'They seem sound enough to get you where you're going,' and motioned me on. All I can do is sit and wait there, hoping he'll figure out that I need something more. It gets really lonely. I get starved, exhausted."

A Man's Response: Out of three billion men on earth, you're the only one who can fill your wife's or girlfriend's emotional tank in this way. How does that make you feel? Now that you know she might often be running on empty, what signals might tell you when she's looking for or needs a fill-up? What difference does it make in your relationship when you affirm her and tell her she's beautiful?

Weekly Challenge: (1) Make a mental or written list of all the things you genuinely find attractive about the woman in your life. [You get bonus points if they're not sex related.] Think about both inner and outer beauty. Find at least three opportunities to mention a few items from your list of her lovely attributes and see how she responds. [Just be sure she never catches you reading them off your shirt sleeve, or you're dead.] (2) Also, raise those relational antennas again, then watch and listen this week for various ways your wife or girlfriend may be asking, "Do you think I'm pretty?" And ensure that you affirm her at those times. (3) Optional: Choose one way, within your budget, to actively encourage [instead of frown on] her desire to invest in her wardrobe, her cosmetics, her jewelry, a spa treatment, or some other beautifying measure.

Someone Once Said...

"Nothing makes a woman more beautiful than the belief she is beautiful." —Sophia Loren

The BIG Idea

One main idea I'm taking away from this week's discussion is…

One way I plan to apply this insight to my relationship is…

ON THE HOME FRONT: LIVING IT WITH HER

Certain questions—"Does this make my hips look big?"—strike fear into the heart of the most confident man. But now you know that what she's really asking is, "Do I still rock your world?" (By the way, the answer to the first is *always,* "Your hips are perfect." And to the second, "More than you can imagine." Whatever you do, don't mix them up.) No matter how many times you've said it or how obvious her inner and outer beauty seems to you, she'll never get enough of hearing that you can't tear your eyes off her.

Wake Up Your Inner Hero

When she brushes aside your compliments ("I'll bet you say that to all your wives."), you may wonder if you've wasted your breath. But what she's really saying is, "Tell me again. Do you really mean it? I *need* you to mean it." The more often you reassure her with specific, sincere compliments, the more she'll come to believe that you really do mean it. And the more it'll become a daily habit on your part that gives her daily delight on her part. Further, as she sees that you only have eyes for her, she'll start to glow with confidence in herself and in you, her protector and hero.

Take the Plunge

This week the questions I'm suggesting are intended not to generate conversation but to help you encourage and build up the woman you love. These are intended only as starting points. You'll want to choose one or two and make them your own so she'll know your words are sincere.

- Have I told you today how absolutely gorgeous you are?
- How did a guy like me end up with a beautiful woman like you?
- Did you know that one of the things I love most about you is
_____?
- Do you have any idea how glad I am that you're mine?
- How am I supposed to concentrate at work when I keep picturing how wonderful you looked this morning?

Note: Our primary focus in this section was on a woman's need to know she's beautiful. But there was another point in this chapter that some of us need to deal with as well. Telling her that she's beautiful becomes meaningless if she feels—or knows—that she's in competition with other women for your attention. Let's be real. Keeping your eyes only for her isn't easy, but the results of giving in to temptation are devastating for both of you. If you're struggling with lust or pornography, I urge you to not brush it off as unimportant or deceive yourself into thinking it will go away. Please check out the many specialized resources available to help you, and perhaps even guide you through a serious conversation with your wife, if necessary. You might want to start at www.pureintimacy.org.

Chapter 8

THE MAN SHE HAD HOPED TO MARRY

What the woman who loves you most,
most wants you to know

> **Weekly Challenge Report:** How often did you
> notice the woman in your life wondering if you
> find her beautiful? What clues did you pick up
> on? How did making a list of her attributes affect
> your interactions with her this week? What were
> the results of your efforts to affirm her beauty?
> (Ooh, that good, huh?)

Recap

Beneath all the differences, the miscommunications, the frustrations… nearly all women wish their husbands or boyfriends knew one basic truth: they deeply need, desire, and respect their men. Your wife or significant other doesn't always know how to show it, but she always feels it. In her eyes, you *are* the hero she had hoped to marry. The woman you love honestly loves and admires you. And you have what it takes to be the leader, protector, friend, and support she needs you to be.

"We've now seen over and over that you can be the only person to change in your relationship and still expect great new beginnings. Your marriage is definitely worth you taking the first step."
—*Jeff, FMO, p. 179*

Key Questions

1. Ninety-three percent of the women in the *For Men Only* survey said they admire their men. It's true. Does the overwhelming number surprise you? Why or why not?

2. When you stop and think about it, what signs do you see in your wife's or girlfriend's words and actions that she *does* need and respect you?

3. Aside from being an irresistibly studly hunk, what have you done to earn her admiration? What do you think she would describe as your greatest assets as her provider, protector, husband, and friend? Where do you think you can improve?

4. Let's say you suspect you're among the unhappy 7 percent—the disrespected minority. What steps can you take to improve your relationship?

Note to leaders and participants: "The Real World" case study has been omitted from this chapter in order to allow everyone the necessary time to thoughtfully complete the final "On the Home Front"—type section on page 71 (even if you haven't been doing the section previously). Please allow time for every group member to complete this exercise in preparation for ongoing application of the insights from *For Men Only.*

A Woman's Perspective: "Yeah, I might wish that my husband did some things differently. But whenever I hear someone else putting him down, I get mad. I guess I instinctively defend him. 'He really is the best thing that ever happened to me,' I sometimes say. You know what? It's true. Why do I not realize he needs to hear that?"

A Man's Response: Your wife or girlfriend almost certainly admires and desires you more than you know; how does that affect your view of her? of yourself? What could you do to make it easier for her to voice her admiration?

> **Ongoing Challenge:** Consider, either with your group or alone, agreeing to the *For Men Only* resolutions on page 73 of this guide. Then tear the page out and post it somewhere as a reminder of some of the things she most needs.

Someone Once Said...

"A great marriage is not when the 'perfect couple' comes together. It is when an imperfect couple learns to enjoy their differences."
—Dave Meurer

A FINAL CHALLENGE FOR "ON THE HOME FRONT": CONTINUING TO LIVE IT WITH HER

So we've learned a few things about the women we love and about women in general. But we're not fooling ourselves; neither of us are experts yet—nor are we likely to be. We'll spend a lifetime learning how to love our women and applying these lessons. But now that you've worked through this book, I hope your wife or girlfriend seems less like a swamp. I hope you're starting to understand the map of her inner self and have gained some relationship tools and skills that will help you navigate in the years ahead.

Wake Up Your Inner Hero

Realizing that you—yes, *you!*—are the hero she hoped to marry has probably fueled your desire to live up to her expectations. And as I've said before, those expectations aren't nearly as unreasonable or impossible as we previously thought. You're fully equipped to win her heart over again every day. We both know the payoff is more than worth the effort.

Take the Plunge

To propel you further down the road to relational bliss (or at least prevent you from wandering back into the swamp), I encourage you to glance back through this guide and identify two or three specific application steps you want to continue working on over the next several weeks:

1. _____

_____

_____

2. _____
   _____
   _____

3. _____
   _____
   _____

I also suggest you establish a plan for follow-up support and accountability, something that will work well for you, that you know will add value going forward. For example, if you've worked through this guide on your own, think of another guy who might be willing to join you in talking through these issues on a regular basis. Or if you're in a discussion group, consider pairing off with another guy in the group and checking in with each other by phone once a week and meeting once a month. Or you may want to schedule one more group meeting in six weeks to see how you're all doing with your commitments. Describe your plan here:

_____
_____
_____

Remember, you're already her hero. And now you have also gained some fantastic skills and knowledge that many guys never grasp. You have the map to her heart. Be encouraged as you continue on the adventure with her, with confidence.

THE *FOR MEN ONLY* RESOLUTIONS

N ow that I better understand the inner life of the woman I love, I will…

1. Assume that her reactions are a natural, logical part of her uniquely feminine nature and will do my part to ensure that she *feels* understood and loved.

2. Frequently reassure her of my love and commitment, even when her insecurity is not my fault.

3. Continue to pursue her in big ways and little—a touch, a note, an occasional mushy compliment—even though I've already caught her.

4. Try not to take it personally when she brings up something old, emotional, or off topic that I think she should be able to just let go of; instead, I will encourage her to talk it out and resolve it…or maybe even take action that will resolve it for her.

5. Realize that providing means lots of things besides money, bring my work hours in line with our shared priorities, and devote the first share of my off-work hours to connecting with her and helping out at home.

6. Set aside the obvious problem—work frustrations, misbehaving kids, manipulative relatives—when she voices an emotional concern and will address the real issue by listening to, acknowledging, and affirming her feelings.

7. Try not to take offense when she says no to sex and will understand that it's probably not about me but about her sexual wiring.

8. Show her affection in nonsexual ways every day, give her time to warm up to the idea of sex, and do my best to help her get full satisfaction from sex. (Okay, I'll brush my teeth and take a shower too.)

9. Tell her often that she's the most exciting, attractive woman in the world to me and will prove it by reserving my eyes only for her.

10. Believe that she respects and admires me, even if she doesn't always show it.

Discover the power to change yourself and your relationships!

The best-selling author of *For Women Only* teams up with her husband to offer men the key to unlocking the mysterious ways of women. Through Shaunti and Jeff Feldhahn's national survey and hundreds of interviews, *For Men Only* reveals what men can do today to improve their relationships. And believe it or not, as Jeff assures men, "It's not splitting the atom."

MULTNOMAH BOOKS

www.mpbooks.com
www.formenonlybook.com